SONGS AND SONNETS

Shane McCrae's most recent books of poetry are *New and Collected Hell* and *The Many Hundreds of the Scent*. He has edited a volume of John Berryman's uncollected Dream Songs, titled *Only Sing*. McCrae has been a finalist for both the T. S. Eliot Prize and the Forward Prize, and his awards include a Lannan Literary Award, a Whiting Writer's Award, and a Michael Marks Award. He has received fellowships from the Guggenheim Foundation, The National Endowment for the Arts, and the New York Foundation for the Arts. He lives in New York City.

Also by Shane McCrae

In Canaan (Rescue Press, 2010)

Mule (Cleveland State University Poetry Center, 2011)

Blood (Noemi Press, 2013)

Nonfiction (Black Lawrence Press, 2014)

Forgiveness Forgiveness (Factory Hollow Press, 2014)

The Animal Too Big to Kill (Persea Books, 2015)

In the Language of My Captor (Wesleyan University Press, 2017)

The Gilded Auction Block (Farrar, Straus and Giroux, 2019)

Sometimes I Never Suffered (Farrar, Straus and Giroux, 2020)

Cain Named the Animal (Farrar, Straus and Giroux, 2022)

Hex and Other Poems (Bad Betty Press, 2022)

Pulling the Chariot of the Sun: A Memoir of a Kidnapping (Scribner, 2023)

The Many Hundreds of the Scent (Farrar, Straus and Giroux, 2023)

New and Collected Hell: A Poem (Corsair, 2025)

Two Appearances After the Resurrection (Omnidawn, 2025)

For Melissa

© 2025, Shane McCrae. All rights reserved; no part of this book may be reproduced by any means without the publisher's permission.

ISBN: 978-1-917617-36-9

The author has asserted their right to be identified as the author of this Work in accordance with the Copyright, Designs and Patents Act 1988

Cover designed by Aaron Kent

Edited by Andre Bagoo

Typeset by Aaron Kent

Broken Sleep Books Ltd
PO BOX 102
Llandysul
SA44 9BG

CONTENTS

THE SULLEN HEART OF THE BEAST	11
BLANK VERSE SONNET ON PURITY	12
BLANK VERSE SONNET ON OUR MYTHS EXCUSE US	13
BLANK VERSE SONNET ON HERE WE GO AGAIN	14
BLANK VERSE SONNET CONCLUDED BY A PURE RHYME AND AN IMPURE RHYME	15
QUATRAINS ON HE MAKES A WINNING ARGUMENT	16
ELIZABETHAN SONNET ON FROM 2004 TO 2023 CLARENCE THOMAS RECEIVED $4 MILLION IN GIFTS	17
BLANK VERSE SONNET ON AMERICA IS LISTENING	18
ELIZABETHAN SONNET ON VIOLATING THE FLAG CODE	19
TRUMP ALONE ON THE MORNING OF HIS SECOND INAUGURATION	20
UPSIDE-DOWN PETRARCHAN SONNET ON THIS IS HOW YOU HANDLE	21
PETRARCHAN SONNET ON A GOLDEN AGE IN ARTS AND CULTURE KASH PATEL PRODUCER	22
NOVEMBER LIGHT, 2023	23
BLANK VERSE SONNET ON HE CONTEMPLATES THE SHORT FILM KNOWN AS "TRUMP GAZA"	25
ELIZABETHAN SONNET ON HE MUSES UPON THE DEAL THAT WASN'T	26
AFTER PIETER BRUEGEL THE ELDER'S *THE HUNTERS IN THE SNOW*	27
ELIZABETHAN SONNET ON TRUMP AS A KING ADDRESSES THE JANUARY SIXERS	28

PETRARCHAN SONNET ON THE ELECTRIFIED SEA	29
PSEUDO-PETRARCHAN SONNET ON HE FIRED SEVERAL MEMBERS OF THE NATIONAL SECURITY COUNCIL AFTER LAURA LOOMER URGED HIM TO DO SO	30
SPENSERIAN SONNET ON HE CONSIDERS NEIGHBORLINESS	31
THINKING OF THE CHILDREN, OR ON STUDENT PROTESTS	32
SONNET WITH WORDS YOU HAVE TO IGNORE	34
SONNET IN WHICH MOST OF THE RHYMES FAIL	35
PETRARCHAN SONNET ON HE TALKS ABOUT THE FIRST ASSASSINATION ATTEMPT	36
ELIZABETHAN SONNET ON HE'S THINKING OF PHOTOSHOP BUT CAN'T REMEMBER THE NAME	37
ELIZABETHAN SONNET ON HE RECALLS HIS TIME AS A STUDENT MUSICIAN AS HE TALKS ABOUT BOMBING IRAN	38
ACKNOWLEDGMENTS	41

*If I don't learn to shut my mouth I'll soon go to hell,
I, Okigbo, town-crier, together with my iron bell.*

— Christopher Okigbo

Songs and Sonnets

Shane McCrae

Broken Sleep Books

THE SULLEN HEART OF THE BEAST

– Washington D. C., January 6th, 2021

The man in the Beast the sullen heart   of the Beast

    Imagines first the wheel unpleasant

    Gripping the wheel to the touch at least

    A little damp he wonders isn't

It skin a little skin   or inside parts

    And gross to touch it either thing

    In blood or sweated on   with warts

    And flakes of shit and he   can't bring

Almost himself to lunge for the steering wheel

    Imagining what it has been

    But how would bloody leather feel

    He thinks   *Like it's alive again*

BLANK VERSE SONNET ON PURITY

America your blood is poisoned Lord
Help you it's poisoned and no God can help you
America nah   what you need is bleach
I read it in a headline bleach   and sunlight
Back when the president was president
America just open up a vein
A big one let   the sunlight in   the bleach

I bet it's gotta feel like when you're hot
So hot you see a bottle of cold water
And it looks *good*   and when you drink it you
Can feel that coldness falling to your belly
America I bet that's how it feels
To clean your blood to   make your insides white
Except the cold is everywhere forever

BLANK VERSE SONNET ON OUR MYTHS EXCUSE US

A cloud of sulfur gas solidifies

Until it isn't gas and every bulge in

The it was   undulating slithering

But floating   cloud is now a face and each

Face its own shade of white   that's how the rallies

Start   then from deep in the earth or near the surface

Clay rises and converges on a smaller

Cloud the crowd's exhalations roiling toxic

The clay encloses it   the cloud the clay

Assumes an old man's shape skin   orange like

A setting sun to burn the cloud apart

A golden   plug on top to trap the stench

But the stench   slithers out the face but you

Can't smell the poison when it's your own breath

BLANK VERSE SONNET ON HERE WE GO AGAIN

America I feel your guilty shrugging

The cotton sliding from your shoulder clos

-er to your throat I feel it   at my throat

America your dry   but not unpleasant

Cottony hands they're sliding from the right

And from the left they're sliding up my chest

From just above my heart and   yes from to

The right of it my heart   feels like a col

-lar tightening feels   like I'm feeling it

For you the iron collar of your shrug

And guilty   yes but guilty like a child

Licking the chocolate from his fingers after

The grocer told him not to steal   and turned

Back to his phone   and would not raise his head

BLANK VERSE SONNET CONCLUDED BY A PURE RHYME AND AN IMPURE RHYME

What happens when I win is what the movie

Said happens what the video okay

Said *The   Creation of a Unified*

Reich that's what happens what   does that mean *reich*

It's German they have done   tremendous things

That's all it means   it's German like the Ger

-man word   for country we are gonna be

One country you America you know

You know   what one means one means no more jobs

Will go to immigrants one means our troops will

Clean up the border unified that's one

You hear it   *one* in the *un* one country un

Country I win one reich a thousand years

From now they won't believe what happened here

QUATRAINS ON HE MAKES A WINNING ARGUMENT

We're gonna win this thing okay we're so
Far we're ahead in states Republicans
Don't ever win they're losers we are go
-ing   to 'cause who can stop us win the wins

Will be so huge you'll   gag on them you'll choke
You'll get so sick of choking   but we'll keep
On winning it's a   folks the system's broke
I didn't break it   while you were asleep

At the wheel wow   some bad   some thug we all
Know who I mean he's not   American
He broke it everything you know I'm tall
-er nobody   at fake news CNN

Will say that stand us   back to back who dunks in
Whose face which one jumps smarter   what I mean is
Jack Smith and all his goons belong in trunks in
The Gulf   here's one about a giant penis

ELIZABETHAN SONNET ON FROM 2004 TO 2023 CLARENCE THOMAS RECEIVED $4 MILLION IN GIFTS

I made as much I almost made as much

Four million on the side as I got paid

Let myself down there   should've made as much

Made more you   either play or you get played

Why should I save a rich man's life for free

I mean it's that's   it isn't it the game

Their money or your life   black folks are free

As scraps of paper   curling in a flame

You only need a breeze and you will fly

God makes the breeze to blow   or you get burned

Friend   but it's not God's fault if you don't fly

What if I hadn't hustled   hadn't learned

From wealthy men   those men affirm my power

You don't have power if no one buys your power

BLANK VERSE SONNET ON AMERICA IS LISTENING

C'mon America who buys a judge

I don't buy judges I just maybe talk

About their kids where   you might hear me talking

Or maybe I don't talk   you saw the mug

-shot right so   I don't need to talk   it's good

The shot one eye is bad the eye looks bad

It's like it's sick you know but no   a very

Respected doctor said I'm healthier

Than any other president   and you

Could hear the shiver in his voice   no I

Don't need to talk   maybe I'll cry   a sin

-gle tear from my bad eye you know   what's tough

It's tough to cry   and just by crying make

Somebody kill whoever made you cry

ELIZABETHAN SONNET ON VIOLATING THE FLAG CODE

How much are we supposed to take the guy in

His yard he had   a sign it said *Fuck Trump*

And so my wife complained she   wasn't whining

But it was like the guy just took a dump

In the middle of our neighborhood just right

There in the street   just took a shit his yard

The street whatever   anyway that might

Have been the end of it but she was scarred

My wife by the   foul mouth on this guy fucking

Filthy the things he said to her I'll tell

You what that guy is lucky   very lucky

I wasn't there   say *Fuck Trump* then   they're all

Cowards you hang   it upside-down when you

Fear for your life   the flag says *Fuck you too*

TRUMP ALONE ON THE MORNING OF HIS SECOND INAUGURATION

You better fucking   shit you fucking better

Pardon those fucking assholes fucking   Fauci

Milley and fucking   Cheney you saw how she

Betrayed her country me you're   gonna let her

Just get away with it   you're an abettor

To it's the   greatest crime   it is   and now the

People won't ever get justice I mean wow the

Depths Joe you   piss on me and you'll get wetter

Than me you piss   on my inaugura-

tion you'll be crawling through the puddle on

Your knees to kiss my fucking knuckles   what

For what   for nothing   *I* have fucking mon-

ey not those pricks   enjoy your fucking   hut

Your dirt   enjoy being good Joe   how's the pay

UPSIDE-DOWN PETRARCHAN SONNET ON THIS IS HOW YOU HANDLE

> *Rather than being attracted to light, researchers believe that artificial lights at night may actually scramble flying insects' innate navigational systems, causing them to flutter in confusion around porch lamps, street lights and other artificial beacons.*
>
> — Christina Larson, Associated Press

our so-called friends   last week the leader of

A major power it's   a conference says

Sir stands up now   this guy he's small   a bug

An insect insects I don't like   his eyes

They're what's the word they're   *bulbous* and he's tug

-ging down his jacket *Sir* says *Sir*   *we love*

You in wherever the hell he comes from right

Especially our women says   *If we*

Owed NATO money   *would you possibly*

Please   *still protect us* now   I love a fight

I tell him *I would tell you*   *pay tonight*

Or I send Putin tanks tomorrow he

Says nothing   but it's in his eyes I see

It he is *dead*   it kills them   bugs   the light

PETRARCHAN SONNET ON A GOLDEN AGE IN ARTS AND CULTURE KASH PATEL PRODUCER

> *At my direction, we are going to make the Kennedy Center in Washington D.C., GREAT AGAIN. I have decided to immediately terminate multiple individuals from the Board of Trustees, including the Chairman, who do not share our Vision for a Golden Age in Arts and Culture. We will soon announce a new Board, with an amazing Chairman, DONALD J. TRUMP!*
>
> — Donald Trump, February 7, 2025

I'm an amazing Chairman I will be

The most amazing   Chairman of the Board

I could have been Sinatra   my voice soared

Over the hostages that   was all me

No tricks   just talking right I tell Kash *See*

What happens when you turn me up   he's floored

It's beautiful I tell him   *Add a chord*

There aren't enough chords Kash says *I agree*

Sir and he turns the knobs the   chord knobs says

You'll hear it   in the final mix I   soar

Over a perfect hostage chord if Hez-

bollah could hear it   truly   peace we've got to

Get it in mosques the speakers if they're not too

Wrecked if we can't   we've got to wreck them more

NOVEMBER LIGHT, 2023

Always but imperceptible
By living eyes the light from things
Events at any distance   inches
Even   the light from things events
Because it has to travel you

See the event   thing after it
Happens   a living person sees
It not to say the   dead would see
Anything quicker see the instant
It happens not to say the dead

See things   events without the aid
Of light but we   the living see
After on Earth an interval
Too brief to notice   things events
On Earth   some stars are dead of course

And how would anybody notice
Perceive the event   thing happening
Before they see it happening
The looked-at thing   event   not touch
The signals have to travel not

Sound   sound is so   much slower children

Do math between the flash and crack

Of the same bolt not smell no   smells

Are slow as air   unless the corpse

Is hidden in the walls unless

The corpse is hidden in the bushes

But maybe   if the corpse is hidden

In light itself   behind a screen

The air the living person breathed

Will take ten thousand lives to reach you

BLANK VERSE SONNET ON HE CONTEMPLATES THE SHORT FILM KNOWN AS "TRUMP GAZA"

The bearded dancers they were my idea

You should have seen the first   cut no you shouldn't

Have it was nasty   sick the beards were rain

-bow and the pink girl's belly wobbled like

It had maracas in it   plus the kid

Running at the beginning was on fire

Burning and smiling   like the schools were back

And a gold god was pissing cash from the sky

You think he's smiling 'cause he doesn't know

He's burning   or he's burning 'cause he's so

Happy he doesn't realize he's burning

I asked the AI it just fixed the cut

And asked me was I satisfied   I was

The AI had made the bearded dancers hot

ELIZABETHAN SONNET ON HE MUSES UPON THE DEAL THAT WASN'T

Well let's be honest who wants genocide

It's bad for whole communities of people

Some people   just won't make a deal   I tried

I said *Your city's shit you   sell it cheap I'll*

Send you your   leaders and your families some

-where nice I've got an island it's a lit

-tle   cold in mind but there's a lot of room

A lot of room sell   Gaza and I'll let

You occupy that green and pleasant place

Bibi will never bother you again

Two birds okay   and the third bird was peace

It would have covered Gaza like an iron

Springtime   a Riviera   what a beauty

I promise you   once we've removed the bodies

AFTER PIETER BRUEGEL THE ELDER'S *THE HUNTERS IN THE SNOW*

The magpie does forever what the four

Crows will   or would in time the magpie flies

A pack of dogs   most whole some tails and more

Whole bodies but they're missing heads and eyes

And ears and tongues and teeth but   they have necks

Sniff hungrily the snow behind the men

Hunters at least one one   of the dogs expects

Hopes   one to eat the strung-up fawn its thin

Forelegs its too short   forelegs stiffened war

-ily between its neck and the dog's teeth

The at least one forever   anywhere

Death is who sniffing   hoping follows death

ELIZABETHAN SONNET ON TRUMP AS A KING ADDRESSES THE JANUARY SIXERS

> *It took the Nazis one month, three weeks, two days, eight hours and 40 minutes to dismantle a constitutional republic.*
>
> — JB Pritzker, February 19, 2025

> *LONG LIVE THE KING!*
>
> — Donald Trump, February 19, 2025

It takes a month that's all it takes it takes

A month a week   a week and then another

I shake the baby till its fat neck breaks

The screaming   woman never was its mother

You know it's true I'll say it till it's true

But till you don't know who said what   our enemy or me   our enemy is you

You fight and then don't die and fight again

When if you die your faith becomes the law

Hungry as law   to eat until it pops

From hunger comes the awe of kings   but awe

Will also take more shaking   then who stops

Your king becoming king and the dead   sing

You sing   *The king is death*   *long live the king*

PETRARCHAN SONNET ON THE ELECTRIFIED SEA

Picture a boat   whatever boat a yacht
Okay real big   don't picture a canoe
No two   -man fishing boat the   sky is blue
Beautiful day   no clouds   and it's just hot
Enough you're shirtless on the deck   you've got
A Diet Coke on the table next to you
Sweating   the can looks beautiful a new
One and the pretty   stewardess right brought
It smiling you're about to drink it

                                 but

The yacht is green folks   powered by a bat
-tery a huge one   and it sinks   now what
'Cause there's a shark too sharks like sun too that
Shark's tan lean hungry you   get eaten or
Get fried   who's left to save the planet for

PSEUDO-PETRARCHAN SONNET ON HE FIRED SEVERAL MEMBERS OF THE NATIONAL SECURITY COUNCIL AFTER LAURA LOOMER URGED HIM TO DO SO

Who knows what women want I think they like

Me right they like me that's what people say

The experts body   language experts they

Tell me decorum experts coaches Mike

Johnson he calls so late   he calls so late

He wakes me up to   ask me does he think

They like me   I can almost hear him blink

When I say *Yes* Laura   participat-

ed in the meeting yes she's very bright

A brilliant   girl a brilliant *woman* right

She had a list of names   she wants to keep

Me safe that's good she tells me   she can't sleep

Thinking about staff loyalty no tyrant

Is loved like that   real women want what *I* want

SPENSERIAN SONNET ON HE CONSIDERS NEIGHBORLINESS

Tariffs are promises oh   man they're sweet

They're little girls in pigtails hugging Ken

In princess dresses high   heels on their feet

You run from that you're not American

And where to   only losers live in Can-

ada in Mexico they've got huge spiders

Tarantulas Americans   are men

Men don't like bugs   men win   men are providers

Okay just look there's   food in the camps   inside there's

Food TV weights the Mexicans they fly

Their pregnant women here in homemade gliders

Who pays for the air they're gliding on   in my

America there's tariffs on the air

America means promise everywhere

THINKING OF THE CHILDREN, OR ON STUDENT PROTESTS

Americans love children the idea of

Sometimes the execution   sometimes one

-On-one we   know which children to steer clear of

But send us Facebook Reels we'll love the   fun

-nily sad kids   in the Facebook Reels we'll love

Our own   with an inspired love then   and pull

Them close as if they each   child were the moth

-Chewed blanket we found in our mother's hall

-way closet when we threw away her things

And hold them close   until we smell their stink

We love our   children while the singer sings

About their fathers beating them   the link

Disappeared or we would have given money

But hearts are money   so we heart the song

The cutest kitten shivers and has runny

Eyes   or at least it can't retract its tongue

And will die smiled-at   love is smiles and cry
-ing   oh the big-eyed kid whose big eye runs
We love that kid those kids heart   each sick eye
And we have tear gas for the healthy ones

SONNET WITH WORDS YOU HAVE TO IGNORE

The gunman in the Uvalde massacre had purchased a hellfire device, which was recovered from one of the classrooms where the massacre took place

— Tim Dickinson

I will not write a poem about their heads

Torn off by hellfire   spring and summer meet

Torn off by hellfire   now   a subject meet

Torn off by hellfire   for a poem   they meet

Torn off by hellfire   first in April meet

Torn off by hellfire   -ing in warm rain meet

Torn off by hellfire   for new life   they meet

Torn off by hellfire   when new life buds   meet

Torn off by hellfire   when it ripens meet

Torn off by hellfire   May through August meet

Torn off by hellfire   green through green   they meet

Torn off by hellfire   till bright gold leaves meet

Torn off by hellfire   ruby leaves   that meet

In crowns on the bigtooth maples their sweet heads

SONNET IN WHICH MOST OF THE RHYMES FAIL

How many now a thousand I can't look

America a thousand still   I said

I couldn't then I looked   how could I not

When I imagine Hell I see the dead

Together in a lake I see a thousand

About a thousand   in a burning lake

The only torment most of us remember

But where we heard of it we don't remember

We us   how many children did we take

And keep are keeping though we're better were

Had voted ourselves better   good enough

To try to give them back and give up slowly

How many now have most of all their lives

Been trapped with us while we were giving up

PETRARCHAN SONNET ON HE TALKS ABOUT THE FIRST ASSASSINATION ATTEMPT

I am my people   say so and it's true

A changed man death has changed me death so close

The bullet would have taken off my nose

If I had turned too   far around and who

Death   lies so flat on roofs he's   look he's too

Close to the roofs to cast a shadow   those

People behind me they my   people chose

People   who maybe were important to

Butler and what's near Butler and where's Butler

People who didn't just look furious

When they were happy   who could wave a sign

I turned because I couldn't hear but   what for

I heard a voice   I didn't know the voice

Until the bullet struck my ear   was mine

ELIZABETHAN SONNET ON HE'S THINKING OF PHOTOSHOP BUT CAN'T REMEMBER THE NAME

I saw my blood and wondered   had I cut her

The woman in the picture agent in

The picture her   I don't remember what her

Name was I must have known it knew it when

Before she rushed the stage to what I guess

Take the next bullet   but I think the guy

Was dead already   how'd they hide the mess

His blood and insides from the pictures I

Was told they hid it   if I knew computers

I'd find the   pictures of the guy myself

I tell my guys   *I want to see the shooter's*

Body   they talk about my "mental health"

Somebody Elon   anybody show

Me how to hide the blood   and then I'll know

ELIZABETHAN SONNET ON HE RECALLS HIS TIME AS A STUDENT MUSICIAN AS HE TALKS ABOUT BOMBING IRAN

I dropped the bunker busters on the mountain

Like who perhaps   no country could have done

I used to play the flute   I watched the wand guy count in

Then counted to a hundred played my one

Note   and then counted to two hundred bowed

And opened up my eyes again and left

I asked a general *What's that sound like*   *Loud*

He said   and walked away   he had a cleft

Chin like a toy   that's what I'll tell whoever

I tell to fire the guy for me I'll say

Fire G.I. Joe you know   I never

Watched   if I watched the crowd I couldn't play

I'd hear a voice   just   shouting in my head

PICTURE THEM NAKED   but I saw them dead

ACKNOWLEDGMENTS

I am grateful to and for my family and friends, and the editors, staffs, and readers of the following journals, in which some of the poems in this pamphlet first appeared: *The American Poetry Review*, *Berlin Lit*, *Literary Matters*, *The New York Review of Books*, *Nimrod*, *Only Poems*, *Poetry*, and *The Sewanee Review*.

"Sonnet with Words You Have to Ignore" appeared on the *Best American Poetry* blog.

LAY OUT YOUR UNREST

www.ingramcontent.com/pod-product-compliance
Lightning Source LLC
LaVergne TN
LVHW041311080426
835510LV00009B/955